7DAY FAST

Understanding God's Plan
Through Faith and Action

Billy Horton

Understanding God's Plan
Through Faith and Action

Billy Horton

╬RICHER Press
An Imprint of Richer Life, LLC

Published and distributed by ╫RICHER Press
An Imprint of Richer Life, LLC

4600 E. Washington Street, Suite 300, Phoenix, Arizona 85034
www.richerlifeassociates.com

Cover Design: Laura Rutt and Epic Print Solutions

Photographs: Billy Horton and Epic Print Solutions

Library of Congress Cataloging-in-Publications Data

Horton, Billy
7 Day Fast: Understanding God's Plan Through Faith and Action
Billy Horton -- 1st edition
p.   cm.
ISBN 978-0-9855699-3-8 (pbk : alk. Paper)
1. Christian 2. Inspiration 3. Reference

2012951142

ISBN 13: 978-0-9855699-3-8
ISBN 10: 0-9855699-3-8

Text set is Adobe Garamond
First edition, October 2012

Printed in the United States of America

ACKNOWLEDGEMENTS

The creation of this book has been an amazing experience and trust me without the help of others it would not have been possible. I truly believe it was written to help people who are going through difficult circumstances and for them to draw nearer to God during these times.

First off I would like to thank Jesus Christ, my Lord and Savior, for giving me the idea and the courage to do this. My life was so different 7 years ago and it has drastically changed for the better when I dedicated my life to serving Him on August 21, 2005. I am also forever indebted to Bill Crawford, the man who helped me along during that time. He was a great example with his actions and words and was always very encouraging. I am grateful that Bill is still influential in my life today.

Thank you to my wife Taleen for giving me the opportunity to write this when our time was so limited with having two young boys and full time jobs. Thank you also to our sons, Connor & Bryce, for being an inspiration during my writings. Being a better daddy to you and taking care of mommy is my number 1 priority. I would also like to thank Momma Horton for always being there and being my #1 fan my whole life. I love you Mom. You are the best.

I would also like to recognize my friends who have been great examples of how a man should treat his wife and raise his kids. A special thanks goes out to Andre, Kory, Mike and Travis. I am constantly watching your interactions and you guys make me strive to be better.

Last, but certainly not least are the people who did all the hard work getting this book published and on the shelf. This includes my publisher RICHER Press, Laura Rutt and Epic Print Solutions for the awesome book cover artwork and David Smith for my website design. All of you are responsible for helping make this a reality and I am so thankful for all the hours you put into it.

DEDICATION

This book is dedicated to my beautiful wife Taleen. She is a woman of God and shows me an example of a selfless life by the way she takes care of our boys in addition to holding down a full time job at our church. She is a true example of a Proverbs 31 woman and I am fortunate to spend the rest of my life with her by my side.

CONTENTS

INTRODUCTION

MY BASEBALL CAREER

*"Fly ball to left field. Larry Herndon races towards the foul line and he...
makes the catch! The crowd goes crazy! The Detroit Tigers are the 1984
World Series Champions!!!"*

This is one of the fondest memories of my childhood. I
started playing baseball in West Branch, Michigan in 1982
when I was 8 years old and in 1984, my team, the Detroit
Tigers dominated baseball. They started out 35-5 that season
and steamrolled the San Diego Padres in the World Series. The
players on that team were my heroes, and I remember fist
pumping and jumping around when Herndon made the final
catch. You see I was captivated by the game of baseball, and it
consumed my every thought.

All I ever wanted to do was play the game that I loved
so much. Growing up I had well over 5,000 baseball cards and
I memorized every one of them. My sisters would cover up the
names of the players and quiz me on who they were. I would
rattle off them off in machine gun fashion and they would just
shake their heads and wonder how in the heck I could do that.
It was simple. I loved it.

When I was 10, I remember playing catch in my front
yard and deciding that I was going to play 20 years in the big
leagues and retire at the age of 40. My plan was to have a big
house out in the country, raise a family and enjoy my quiet life.
Well, I'm in the game, but not nearly how I thought I would
be.

In the fall of 1986, I moved away from everything I've
ever known in the small country town in Michigan, to the

desert in Glendale, Arizona. I was in 8th grade and I went from Billy Horton, West Branch Little League MVP, to the skinny pale kid with freckles. I did not fit in and hated pretty much everything about my new home.

I attended Cactus High School the next year and was cut from the freshman baseball team. I was demoralized. I started going to the weight room, got stronger and made the junior varsity team the next year. I was stuck on JV my junior year as well, but finally made Varsity my senior year and was offered a handful of college scholarships to some small universities scattered around the country. Even though I made a lot of good friends, I still didn't like Arizona. So, leaving the state was something I wanted to do.

During the summer of 1991, I chose to attend Spring Hill College in Mobile, Alabama and spent the next four years of my life in the South. I wasn't a great player, but I knew that there were some teams interested in me due to my arm strength and athletic ability. I was hoping someone would use a late round pick on me in 1995, but unfortunately I went undrafted. In order to fulfill my dream of one day being a big leaguer, I needed to get to work and find a way to get picked up. I was an infielder most of my life, but my bat wasn't carrying me so I had to learn a new position, catcher.

It was a tough road, but after a lot of hard work, I signed my first pro contract with an Independent team in 1996, but I never ended up playing that year. I got my first chance to play pro ball in 1997 and bounced around with various Independent teams over the next 3 years. I did go to Spring Training with the White Sox in 1999 and the Angels in 2000, but never played in a big league game. I hung up my spikes when I was 26 years old and even though I had a degree in

Marketing, I still loved the game, so I decided to go into coaching.

I've coached at almost every level of youth baseball, from Little League to High School. I founded the baseball training organization, Cactus Athletic Camps in 2006 and in 2007 I started the Arizona Baseball League, which is a youth baseball league for 8 to 16 year olds. In the summer of 2011, I coached in a Collegiate Summer Wood Bat League. However, nothing really fulfilled me baseball wise. The hardest part of all of this was that I was working extremely hard and putting in a lot of hours, but I was not able to provide enough income to pay the bills. When I played, my goal was to be at the highest level of the game --- professional baseball. I was able to attain it as a player and now the desire for me to do it as a coach was burning like an inferno inside me.

I have worked for the Arizona Diamondbacks, Chicago White Sox and Texas Rangers in different capacities in the past, but never as a minor league coach. I knew it was going to be a long shot, but in August of 2011 I started contacting all 30 teams via phone and email to try and find a minor league hitting coach job. Each month from August through November, I repeated the process, slimming down the teams as they said no.

I went into this knowing it was going to be tough, so my mindset was that a "no" from one team, just meant that another team will eventually say "yes." If coaching pro baseball was in God's plan for me and my family, then I believed it would happen. I had to continue to remind myself that His timing is always perfect, even though I was growing impatient and nervous as the calendar kept creeping closer to the end of the year. I had to put my full trust in the Lord and the plan He had for my young family.

11

THE FAST

By definition, a fast is when you abstain entirely from or limit food, especially as a religious observance. My first fast was back in the fall of 2002 and I have been consistently doing this once per month since 2006. I normally limit myself to just water and spend more time in prayer throughout the day. I have never fasted for longer than 2 days and I have only done that one time when a group of us at church did it together.

I was out walking my dogs on Halloween night. I had a lot on my mind and I normally get my best ideas and have some solid prayer time when the mutts and I take off for a half hour or so. My heart was heavy because our family's finances were at an all-time low. I had been searching for a minor league baseball coaching job for the past 3 months and had not heard much back from any of the teams. One of my friends, Derin McMains, is a coach with the San Francisco Giants and he told me a little while back there was a position with them in Rookie Ball and that he would put a good word in for me.

On October 26th my wife, Taleen, and I decided that we would pray specifically for this job with the Giants while we still worked hard to find one with any team that would acknowledge my resume. She decided to fast for three days, while I went for my usual one. The next day Derin spoke at our teenage athletic ministry meeting, better known as Teen Impact, and he let me know that the position we were praying for had been filled. However, he also told me that another position had surfaced, and he let the Giants know that I would be a great candidate for it. He thought that I might hear something within a week, but no promises.

I called Taleen after our meeting and her spirit soared! She was so excited and it gave her a boost as she entered her second day of fasting. What I didn't tell you is that this was her first real fast in at least 3 years because of the birth of our two sons, Connor who recently turned 3, and Bryce who just had his first birthday. She had just stopped nursing Bryce so she felt confident to begin fasting again. What I saw her go through in the next 2 days gave me so much more respect for her and also made me feel guilty as I was grubbing on dinner with the boys as she sipped water at the table with us. To top it off her monthly cycle hit her on the 3rd day, so she was tore up physically and mentally. I felt about 2 feet tall.

So, as I am walking Harley and Bocephus on that cool October night, I feel the Lord tugging at me, challenging me to lead my family. If my wife can go three days I can do at least that much. We had not heard back from the Giants yet, but it had only been a couple of days.

I made a commitment that night to God that I would consume no solid food for 7 days, but that I would allow myself to have more than just water. This included milk, juice, tea and 2 protein shakes per day. I felt like I would need some type of additional nourishment because I am so active in my job. I also had a clause in my agreement with God [I think He smiled as I tried to play sports agent with him] that if I received a job within the 7 days that I would go one additional day after I agree to the coaching position. Therefore if the Giants called and offered me the job 3 days in, I would fast one more day in Thanksgiving to the Lord for his awesome provision.

By the time day 4 had rolled around, I had not heard back from any teams so I took a late morning walk with the dogs. It was this point I decided that I was going 7 days no matter what and I would chronicle everything that happened during the fast.

THE BOOK

7 Day Fast: Understanding God's Plan Through Faith and Action is a book that reveals a lot about me, my faith and how our actions and faith can help us understand God's plan for our life.

The book chronicles my 7 day fast that began on October 31st, 2011. The chronicle itself is actually a complete "diary" of what I experienced, how I felt, and the actions I took each day to realize my goal of strengthening my faith and preparing myself for what the Lord had planned for our family during this very difficult economic time.

As I wrote a summary of each day's activity, I kept focusing on how the struggle I was going through would one day help others. My wife and I both run bible studies and I figured my notes would end up one day helping us come up with ideas for future messages. As I continued to write and I saw the content growing, I realized that this was evolving into a book with a message that can help others gain a sense of how faith and action can clarify God's plan for their lives.

In **7 Day Fast,** I openly share with you:

- My personality, mind-set under pressure and my family life during the 7 days;

- How I managed my personal life and my emotions during this period;

- How I thought through my career dilemma and made important decisions on how to approach the situation;

- The actions I took to strengthen my chances for returning to professional baseball; and

- The spiritually-driven action I took to strengthen my faith in God and to allow His plan for my family to be revealed.

Each day's chronicle is an emotional and revealing look into my life. You will see interactions I have with my family and the frustrations that come when pressure is applied to one's life. When the heat is on, you find out what's inside of you and sometimes you don't like what comes out. However, these are exactly the things that the Lord wants you to work on. They become refining moments in our life and as we overcome them, we become stronger and God will be able to use us to glorify His kingdom in a greater way. I believe it is how God slowly reveals His plan for us.

Words are great, but if you are not walking out the Christian life, your words are meaningless. If you are going to talk the talk, then you have to walk the walk. *7 Day Fast* gives you a good example of how I walk out my faith. As my good friend Andre says "Real recognizes real." In this book, I keep it real.

At the end of each day's chronicle, I share with you what I call an "afterword". It is simply a brief re-cap of what I experienced during the day. I also list three verses of the bible which address the range of emotions I went through that day. The actual text of the verses is located in the "Glossary of Bible Verses" toward the end of the book.

What you are about to read is what I went through. I hope **7 Day Fast** encourages and inspires you to trust God with your life. Allow Him to *drive* and *you sit shotgun*. The book is designed to help you see how being faithful and taking the personal and professional actions required to be successful, in whatever you do, will reveal God's plan for your life.

"You see that his faith and his actions were working together, and his faith was made complete by what he did" - James 2:22

DAY ONE

THE FAST BEGINS that night with the dogs during the walk. Therefore, the meal I consumed a couple of hours earlier would be my last solid meal until dinner on Monday, November 7th. All I can think of as I wake up is holy cow, what did I just get myself into?

The day starts off normal with the craziness of having 2 young boys and 2 dogs. I had re-seeded the back yard with winter grass the week before so the mutts are not allowed back there. I have to put them on leashes as they take care of their business in the front of the house. Of course, Connor wants to come out and help and Bryce is frustrated as we close the door and he is forced to watch from the window. Mommy just woke up and she wants quiet and coffee---not gonna happen.

We get through breakfast with limited food fights and everyone but me seems well nourished, including Bo who lies under the table and eats the droppings that he receives from the young men we are raising. Taleen works at our church and they have their big staff meeting every Tuesday from 9am-12pm, which is great for me because the boys go with her. The church provides free child care on occasions such as this for all employees which gives me time to work from home. However, on this day, the person who was supposed to watch the kids called in sick, which means the boys are at home with me. So this is the way this fast is going to begin --- great, can't wait to see how this week goes.

I unfortunately expect the worst. So, in order to get out of the house for a while the boys and I take the dogs for a walk. This is no easy task as I have a dog leash in each hand and both boys in a double stroller. To top it off Bo came down with valley fever last month and therefore he can only go one lap around the neighborhood because of his strength being sapped. Connor gets restless after I drop Bo off at home after our first lap, so he is now on foot and holding Harley's leash. All it takes is one stray dog to come booking around the corner and this walk is going to turn ugly, because Harley will probably end up chasing the dog and drag Connor down the street. Our second lap is uneventful. So, I decide to go back home and stop while I'm ahead. I'm also very thirsty at this point and I need something to drink. Connor ends up dropping his pants and peeing on the tree in our front yard. Good thing Mom's not home.

The boys end up being very well behaved the rest of the morning and I am encouraged that this is going to be the start to a great day. I actually get some work done in the office while they hang out by the front window for an hour. I am feeling satisfied that I was able to accomplish anything with both boys being awake so we end up going into the living room and playing with some balls and trucks on the floor. Taleen shoots me a text around 11:15 to check up on us and is encouraged that things are going well. I think she was terrified that it was going to be a disaster this morning because I was used to having time to myself and I would get frustrated by the boys being home. So far, so good on day one.

Taleen gets home around 1pm and I am relieved of my parenting duties. I can't seem to get my mind off the Giants, but I have to get some work done before I leave for the batting cage. I take care of some emails and paperwork, then I begin to surf the internet looking for any indications of openings with one of the Major League teams. The Padres and Angels just recently hired new general managers and rumor is there is going to be some coaching jobs available with them. I work as long as I can, then take off for my lesson at the cage with my newest client, a 15 year old named Nick.

His grandma has hired me to work with him on his hitting as he is planning on trying out for the JV team over at Shadow Mountain High School this coming spring. Nick's grandma, is a no nonsense, tell it like it is kind of lady. My favorite. I don't want a bunch of fluff. Give me black and white. I am not a fan of grey.

Nick enters the cage and starts smacking balls off the tee. He's country strong, but all upper body. We go over some technique about utilizing his core and lower body and BOOM, the ball instantly sounds different off his bat. His hands are getting tore up at the 45 minute mark, so we decide to throw a little to see what his arm looks like. The kid has some ability and with some refinement has a chance to be a decent player. We agree to meet again next week and after chugging more water, I am heading back home to watch my family eat.

It's my second chocolate protein shake of the day and I am feeling pretty good. The family sits down to dinner and after a non-eventful night the boys go to bed. Taleen and I stay up to do some work and I come across an article online that says the Seattle Mariners have hired a new Farm Director. This is the person who has a lot of say in who gets hired as a minor league coach, so I shoot him a quick email and hope that something hits. The previous person in that position apparently took a coaching job within the organization, so I am hoping they are shaking things up a bit since they had a terrible season this year. I also shoot a follow up email to the Orioles to see how things are going over there. Man, I need a job.

I finish up and try to get to bed at a decent hour. Bryce has not been consistently sleeping through the night yet, so I am praying that he will. I'm not sure how I will react to getting woken up at 3am by a crying 1 year old. Taleen woke up in the middle of the night for at least 9 months to breast feed him, so I am now on Bryce patrol. For the past few months he has been getting up a couple of times and I don't know what it feels like to sleep through the night anymore. I now understand what she went through and not getting good sleep puts me in a bad mood. Lord, give me favor.

Before I go to bed I open the bible. This is something I try to do every night to clear my mind before I go to sleep. I open up to Psalm 25, which talks about a plea for deliverance and forgiveness. This leads me to ask the Lord to show me anything that I need to work on so I can purify myself during this fast. If there is sin in my life, show me so I can repent of it. I don't want anything standing in the way of my victory!

AFTERWORD

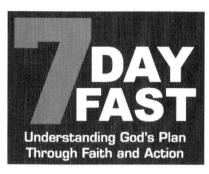

I had fasted a day or two in the past, but not for seven days straight. I was unsure what to expect. However, I had no doubt that taking this particular action was the right thing to do for my family. By the end of the day, I was encouraged by the fact that I had the faith to enter into this period of fasting and that Taleen was there to support me and help keep me focused.

Biblical Points to Consider
While Seeking to Understand God's Plan

Unsure: Proverbs 3:5, 6

Doubtful: Mark 11:23, 24

Encouraged: 2 Thessalonians 3:16

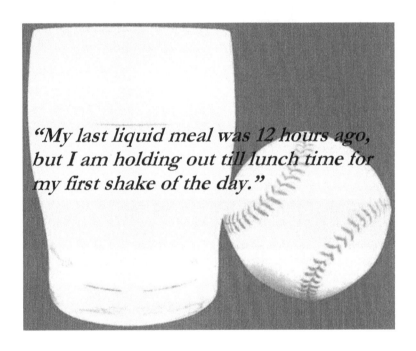

"*My last liquid meal was 12 hours ago, but I am holding out till lunch time for my first shake of the day.*"

DAY TWO

IT'S 3AM AND GUESS who's awake, Mr. Bryce. I am dreading this interaction, but I tell myself to stay positive and immediately start to pray as I pick him up out of his crib. I walk to the living room and rock him for about 10 minutes and he falls back to sleep. Thank you, Jesus. It's back to bed for me, a crowded one at that, since Connor has decided to join us. Bryce woke him up so now this 30 pound generator is in-between T and I. He tends to sprawl out and shove his big ol' feet in my back, but at this point I am just happy to be back under the covers.

It's Wednesday, which is a school day for The CoHo, one of our nicknames for Connor. My body is hurting a little and I am feeling dehydrated. My last liquid meal was 12 hours ago, but I am holding out till lunch time for my first shake of the day. Connor is extra hyper this morning as he crushes his French toast and my head is starting to hurt. Taleen wants to

23

work out this morning so I take both boys with me in the truck and drop Connor off. Bryce falls asleep in his car seat, which is awesome, because now I can come straight back home and get to work. Taleen still has 10 minutes left in her exercise video that she is sweating profusely to in the living room, so I take Bryce with me into our office here at the house and get to work.

Much like the day before I sift through emails, paperwork and count up the registrations for our winter baseball league that starts on November 28th. Numbers are pretty low, which is discouraging. On top of that the phone is not ringing and I am starting to doubt that it will. I get an email back from the Mariners organization that tells me they are fully staffed, but will keep me on file. My mind goes to bad places and I start to wonder what in the heck am I going to do to provide for my family. Taleen's job at the church and the baseball camp business I run is not generating enough revenue for us to live on. I want to provide for them so badly and I start to get mad and frustrated. I need a break from the office and the only thing on my mind right now is drinking a shake. I get into some good prayer time with the Lord and start to feel a little bit better.

Taleen had taken Bryce with her on some errands and he was in his car seat for a while. Noon time rolls around and it's time to go pick up Connor. So, I decide to get him myself and allow her and Bryce to stay home and play in the living room. Connor's school is pretty cool and everyone who works there seems to be very nice. He tells me about his day, as well as a 3 year old can, and on our way home we go do one of his favorite things---look at the "horsies". We live near an area where there are a lot of horse properties and Connor loves to watch them run. Every day Taleen or I take him by these homes and while he is watching them trot around we pray that one day we will be able to provide a home like this for our family.

I get home and the boys sit down for lunch with Momma. I don't want to go back in the office so I spend some time with everyone before I take off for the rest of the day. I have two pitching lessons lined up at a local park, a meeting at Chase Field and then baseball practice until 9pm. It's a long afternoon and I am running between 3 locations, but I am happy to be out of the house and going to the field. It's a place where I am confident and hitting ground balls brings me a certain sense of peace. Before I leave the house I look in the backyard to see my grass coming in spotty due to birds eating some of the seed and a big rainstorm that washed some of it away last week. This just bums be out more so instead of dwelling on this, I give everyone a kiss and jump in the truck.

My first hurler is Adam, a 17 year old left handed pitcher. He is a centerfielder by trade, but he wants to pitch to increase his chance of getting a college scholarship or being drafted by a Major League team. This is our ninth lesson and his main struggle is with his command. He throws a lot of pitches up and in to left handed batters and his last pitching coach was pretty hard on him. His dad is paying good money for me to work with him and we need it, so I have to not only do a good job, but also stay positive as he sends another missile off the backstop behind me. I am pretty sure that he thinks about his last bad pitch versus believing that he will throw a strike the next time he toes the rubber. We talk, make some mechanical adjustments and I encourage him to throw everything down the middle of the plate. Don't try and work the corners. Allow the different grips you are using dictate where the ball will end up. He starts to consistently throw his 2 seam & 4 seam fastballs for strikes now and the curve we just added is pretty darn good. His changeup needs work, but if he can master it, he has a chance to be pretty good. The session ends up very positive and we look forward to meeting again next Monday.

The next pitcher I am working with is Christian, a 12 year old whose Dad has a background in law enforcement. William is a great guy and is a very positive parent. Christian played in our baseball league last year and his dad always sat in the catbird seat behind home plate during the season encouraging both teams and coaches alike. I have been drinking a lot of water and at this point I need to find a bathroom. There are none in the area and William jokes with me and says to do my best to "conceal with intent". We both know this is a bad idea, so I decide to just suck it up and go to a gas station later. Christian and I throw some long toss to start the lesson and this ends up biting me in the butt. He just finished playing football and his arm is not ready for this. The session goes well, but he flames out early due to some triceps fatigue and we finish up by concentrating on some core strengthening exercises. I need to change out of my baseball gear and find somewhere to relieve myself and luckily there is a bathroom on our way out of the park. Five minutes later and I am a new man jumping in the truck heading to Chase Field, the home of the Arizona Diamondbacks.

Right before I leave I blend up my second shake of the day. This one is clumpy, watery and to be honest a little nasty. Man, when all you get is 2 shakes a day they better be good and this one is disappointing. To top it off I spill milk in the truck and my pulse is starting to rise. I give Taleen a call to check up on the family and everything is good on their end which makes me feel better. I don't know what to expect at this meeting, but I am hoping to make some business contacts out of it. My neighbor, Tom, puts on a lot of non-baseball events at Chase and he is the one who invited me. His clients are out on the field and there is food and different random events going on. Some people are taking batting practice at home plate off a softball machine, while others pose for photos in front of a green screen with funky clothing and hats. Someone please shoot me in the face. I'm not a fan of small talk in general and the people in the leopard print and zebra striped hats are really starting to bug me. My attitude could not be worse. I feel like this is a complete waste of time. So, after I stick around for 30 minutes out of respect for Tom, I bolt out of there and change back into my baseball gear in the parking garage. Off to practice at Roadrunner Park.

The three hour practice started at 6pm and I get to the park around 7:15. I have three other coaches running things and I arrive just in time to do one of my favorite things, hit ground balls to the infielders. The crack of the wooden fungo and the rhythm of the infielders throwing to the bases bring me a sense of peace. I finish hitting and go talk to some of the parents watching practice. That's when I realize what the temperature is tonight. When I left the house I dressed appropriately for afternoon baseball lessons in the sun, not evening practice under the lights. It's cold and when I am not moving around it is almost unbearable. I jump in to throw some batting practice around 8:30 to get my blood flowing again and at 9 o'clock we saddle up and get outta dodge. I am feeling pretty good physically and looking forward to thawing out in the truck.

Taleen is still awake when I get home and we get a chance to hang out. We are both discouraged that the Giants haven't called. We discuss if I should call them to find out what the status is. My mind is racing so I stay awake for a while longer risking the Bryce factor and pray that he sleeps through the night. I still need to get in the Word so I open up the bible to a random Psalm and come across number 74. This Psalm is a plea for relief from oppressors. I take it to heart and ask the Lord to deliver us from the financial hardship we are in and to bless us with this job. If it's not the Giants, then please grant us favor elsewhere.

AFTERWORD

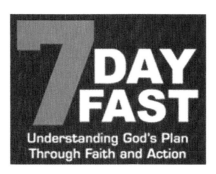

I have been frustrated with things in the past but the level of frustration I was beginning to feel regarding the job opportunity with the Giants was something new. I was becoming more judgmental --- spotty grass and spilled milk should be the least of my concerns. However, the time I spend at the ball park doing what comes natural seems to always calm me down and bring me peace.

Biblical Points to Consider
While Seeking to Understand God's Plan

Frustrated: Psalm 119:10,11

Judgmental: Luke 6:37

Peaceful: Psalm 29:11

"Breakfast is a big struggle, as I am coming to realize that the mornings are the toughest time for me. No sustenance for a half day has sapped my energy even after a decent night's sleep."

DAY THREE

IT'S 3AM AND WHAMMO, I get hit in the face with a baby screaming in the monitor on my nightstand. Bryce is awake and he wants everyone to know it. I am feeling very dehydrated when I roll out of bed. I start praying that the Lord will give me grace and Bryce will go back to sleep without a fight. After about 10 minutes of rocking him I start feeling very weak. I go for a couple more laps around the living room and then lay him back in his crib, praying that he stays asleep. I let Taleen know that if he wakes up, I need her to take over. Bryce starts crying almost immediately after I tell her this and she takes one for the team as I crash back onto my side of the bed. Connor joins me and I get a few more hours of shut eye.

At about 6am BroHo, also known as Bryce, wakes us all up and I find out that Taleen had to jump in the car to get him to fall asleep. She said the process was about an hour and a half long, so I felt pretty bad. Being the amazing wife that she is, she shrugged it off and told me that she was proud that I was staying strong in my fast. She knows I have never gone more than 48 hours before and this was new territory for me.

Breakfast is a big struggle, as I am coming to realize that the mornings are the toughest time for me. No sustenance for a half day has sapped my energy even after a decent night's sleep. Taleen and the rest of the church staff have an event at a local Christian school, which means free child care for us. Thank you Jesus! I can't handle the boys this morning and I have no lessons today so I will be home all day long. Taleen leaves early to go to the school. I need to drop them off with the sitter at our church and after wrestling the boys and dealing with Connor saying no to me about a dozen times, I leave them with Ms. Trini.

On my way home I consider calling someone in the Giants organization to get an update, but I decide not to. Taleen and I have been studying the book of Daniel together recently and in the footnotes of Chapter 10, Verses 12 & 13 it talks about not expecting God's answers to come too easily or quickly. It also states that prayer may be challenged by evil forces, so we should pray fervently and earnestly and then expect God to answer at the right time. Every time the phone rings I feel like I'm a 15 year old girl waiting for the boy she likes to call her, and when it's not him she gets totally deflated. My emotions are a mess and I have to get a grip. Man, being a girl sucks.

I go back home, do some work, and then get word that Taleen is not able to pick up the boys in time. I blend up a chocolate shake on my way out the door, snatch them up from church, and start to drive around hoping that they will both fall asleep so I can have some quiet time to do work. During the drive, I call one of my best friends who is a minor league hitting coach with the Pirates. His name is Kory DeHaan and we have been coaching together at camps and in our baseball league for the past 5 years. Kory is also a strong Christian, great husband and wonderful father of 3 little girls. So, I respect his opinion a lot. He had a tough time when he got back into pro baseball three years ago and I wanted to find out what he thought I should do at this point. His advice, wait and be patient on the Lord. At the same time, I needed to hear it, but didn't want to hear it. I'm a total mess.

At this point I decide to allow a team to contact me and leave it all up to God. The boys don't go to sleep, but Taleen gets home not too long after I arrive at the house. She takes over and I start plugging away in the office doing everything I can to keep my mind off of the Giants and get work done. This was the work that I have been putting off to the side for weeks. There is no relief in the form of going to the field. I am too weak physically to go to the gym and work out. That is my other place of solitude. For 90 minutes I play Christian rock music and get a good pump while I also pray. I seem to get ideas in the squat rack, which is pretty random, but I'm not a normal guy. Things come to me when I am out cruising the neighborhood with the canines and when I'm beating the crap out of myself with a strait bar and 4 big wheels laying across my shoulders. Anyway, I plug away in the office until I see that Taleen needs help with the boys as she is trying to prepare dinner. Bryce is on her leg near the oven and Connor is showing signs of coming down with a cold as he lies on the couch taking a nap. Oh, Lord, don't add this to our week.

Connor is a great little boy. He's very bright and strong as well. Everyone was warning us about the "terrible twos" that kids go through, but Connor was very calm during that time. However, now that he is three we have been dealing with a recent string of disobedience. Like most people he gets grumpy when he is sick so I'm praying this is not serious.

Lasagna. Meaty and juicy with layers of decadent pasta and I get none of it. Earlier in the day I went to the bathroom scale and found my weight had dropped to 183. I started the fast at 194, so I was pretty shocked when I when I saw the number. I talk to Taleen and we discuss whether or not I should add some peanut butter to my chocolate shake. I love chocolate, but after 3 days and 5 shakes, it's getting old and it's the only meal supplement powder we have aside from the fruit flavored one, which is Taleen's favorite. I make the decision with a confident heart that I am not cheating on my fast with the pb, and indulge in the goodness that was my dinner. It wasn't the Italian feast the rest of the family had (let's be honest, it was frozen lasagna so I wasn't missing much), but it tasted good and I had no check in my spirit. One thing I have learned in the past is that you can get very legalistic as a Christian, so it is important to go to God with what is on your heart. It's about your relationship with him, not being religious. I would be visiting the pantry again during this fast and making a date with the tan creamy deliciousness that peanut butter is. High protein, good fat and low in sugar. Tough to beat.

Dinner concludes with some flying pasta and Bocephus does his best impression of one of those dogs you see on ESPN flying through the air grabbing Frisbees as they jump off of a dock over seven logs in the water. Connor now has a runny nose, cough and watery eyes. We don't think he should sleep in the same room as Bryce tonight, so he crashes out on the couch and I fall asleep on the floor next to him reading baseball articles on my phone. I wake up with a stiff neck and my body feels like it did the day after catching an extra-inning game. I let the dogs out and go in the kitchen to read the bible under the stove light so I don't disrupt Connor. I am really tired so I flip to an area where I know that the Psalms are pretty short. I come across Psalm 128 which is only 6 verses long, but is very powerful. It is all about the blessings of those who fear the Lord. Man could we use some of those. I end the night praying that both boys don't wake up until 6am.

AFTERWORD

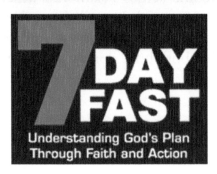

*After three days of fasting, I was beginning to feel a little weak ---
especially in the mornings. But, when I see all that Taleen does on a
routine basis to keep the family going, it strengthens me both physically
as well as mentally. I did notice, however that I was becoming more and
more anxious about the job opportunity with the Giants. To my
surprise, as I moved deeper into my fast, I was becoming more confident
in my decisions and more trusting in my faith. I knew that God's plan
would be the right plan for me and my family.*

Biblical Points to Consider
While Seeking to Understand God's Plan

Weak: 2 Corinthians 12:9

Anxious: Philippians 4:6

Trusting: Psalm 28:7

"Who is wise and understanding among you? Let them show it by their good life, by deeds done in the humility that comes from wisdom." - James 3:13

"I realized that my flesh is weak, but the Lord is stretching my faith to bring me to a new place of strength so that He can rely on me to minister to others at a higher level."

DAY FOUR

IT'S 2AM AND DO YOU know where Billy is? Still asleep. I think I hear Bryce crying and in the morning I come to find out that he had been crying, but Taleen took care of it. This time it was only a short term rocking session. Bryce went back into his crib and she was able to crawl back to bed with the two of us. Yep, around midnight Connor left the couch and came into our bedroom. So, now we have three in the bed again. I was able to stay in bed all night, but it was broken, nasty sleep because Connor's horse-like cough had both Taleen and I awake multiple times. He also ended up nearly lying sideways which turned the three of us into a capital letter "H". Terrible.

This was my worst morning. I felt like I was in a wrestling match with 2 sumo wrestlers and I was caught in-between them as they smacked their bellies together. I am tired, hungry, and impatient and Taleen has to leave for a breakfast meeting with a bunch of women from church at 8am. I am also starting to feel a little something in my sinuses, so I grab a mug of raspberry pomegranate tee. This did not hit the spot. By the time I am finishing it, Taleen is long gone and I have wiped Connor's nose 10 times. He is grumpy, not listening and Bryce is all over the place. I just want some peace and quiet and all they want to do is play and watch animal videos.

I attempt to log on to my laptop to check my emails, which was a huge mistake. The boys are running around like crazy and even though I feel the Lord encouraging me to go play with them, I am not in the right frame of mind to do so. Instead I get frustrated, yell and administer the rod to Connor for not obeying me when I ask him to stop throwing toys. I eventually leave the office and sit on the floor and ask the boys to just be quiet. Of course, they are not capable of doing this, so I sip some water and do my best to stay patient.

It's around 9:15am now and I am exhausted. I decide to grab some chai iced tea from the pantry and make myself a little pick me up. I did the same thing on Wednesday and felt better afterwards. As I am slugging this down, I decide to see the nutritional value of what I am consuming. When I see that the serving has 22 grams of sugar, I am fuming! I realize that my body is not taking in a whole lot it, so it will store whatever it can get. The shakes I am drinking are top notch nutritionally and the skim milk I drink with it is good for me as well. I am now bitter and Taleen is late getting home from her breakfast meeting. I gotta get out of the house.

She gets home about 9:45am and apologizes for being late. It was only 15 minutes, but it felt like forever. She takes the boys in the car for a ride to get Bryce to fall asleep for his afternoon nap. This allows me to take the dogs for a walk, which is gigantic for my mental health. The night before my mind went to the scripture in the bible that talks about self-discipline. In 1st Corinthians 9:27, it says "I strike a blow to my body and make it my slave so that after I have preached to others, I myself will not be disqualified for the prize." The walk triggered the memory and it was at this point that I decided, regardless of whether I received a job offer prior to end of the 7 days or not, that I would make my body my slave and go the full 7 days for the fast. I realized that my flesh is weak, but the Lord is stretching my faith to bring me to a new place of strength so that He can rely on me to minister to others at a higher level. I want this job more that you can imagine, but being a better father, husband an example of a Christian man is more important than where the Lord will place me in the workforce. I also made the decision to write down everything that I was going through during the fast in hopes that it would one day help others. That is what you are reading now.

During our walk Taleen drives by us in the car to let us know that Bryce is asleep and that she is taking Connor to the doctor to get him checked out. We are concerned that he may have an ear infection and since its Friday, we want to find out today, versus waiting until Monday. The dogs and I get home and Taleen takes off with Connor. Bryce is asleep in his car seat, so I can get some work done. I am really encouraged about journaling everything that has happened so far. I need to go from memory on the first 3 days of the fast so I start typing away and as I am halfway through day 2, Bryce wakes up. I am really flying at this point and I don't want to stop, but I have to take care of him. Priorities I tell myself, priorities.

Lucky for me, Taleen gets home within ten minutes of Bryce waking up, which allows me to get back to work on the journal. Connor has what seems to be a common cold and he ends up falling asleep on the couch. As I am typing, I am asking Taleen questions to make sure that I have all the events right that happened over the first 3 days. About an hour later she lets me know that she would like to go for a 30 minute run, and then boom, Connor wakes up in a terrible mood. She handles the boys while I blend up a chocolate peanut butter shake for lunch, and after Connor falls back asleep in her lap on the couch, she takes off for her run.

I am determined to finish up all 3 days before I have to leave for the batting cage at 4pm. So, I bring Bryce in the office with me. In order to keep him occupied I give him a couple of calculators, old envelopes, one of my shoes and some random sheets of paper. By God's grace, it works and I am able to write almost the entire time she is gone. I continue this for a couple more hours and around 3:30pm I shut the computer down, get my stuff together for the rest of the day and take the dogs out front for another bathroom break. Taleen takes the boys to Target to go shopping for some essentials which gives the dogs the house to themselves ---sweet silence for the mutts.

I am in the truck about 4:15pm and I am heading to the batting cage for a hitting lesson with Jackson and his buddy Andy. They are both 13 years old and Jackson has been coming to camps and doing lessons with me for about 4 years. Andy is not that well off, so Jackson's dad pays for him to play in our league, attend our camps and tag along for lessons once in a while. Jackson had never played baseball before he came to our Thanksgiving camp back in 2007, so it's been awesome to see him progress. His Mom passed away earlier this year so I have a soft spot for this family. I talk to his Dad on a pretty regular basis. The boys smack the ball around the cage for an hour and as I look outside the windows of the facility I see the tree branches bending sideways. Not a good outlook for our game tonight. I had already blended my shake at home before I left and, with Taleen's blessing, I tried the fruit flavored one. It's dark green and looks like algae, but the taste is good and it's not chocolate. I don't have a whole lot of options right now so green sludge is a welcoming sight to my eyes and pleasing to my stomach.

I jump in my truck and head to Roadrunner Park. The wind is blowing pretty hard and my cell phone is buzzing away with phone calls & text messages wondering if the game is still on. People in Arizona are very spoiled with our weather so whenever a cloud pops in the sky they tend to freak out. This evening we play against my good buddy Jon Huizinga. He is a phenomenal pitching coach and a great guy. The name of our league is the Arizona Baseball League and I founded it back in November 2008. All of the head coaches have professional baseball experience, which is a big draw for the kids. I get to the field, Jon & I have a few laughs, talk about our starting pitchers and comment on how nice it is out. We are both originally from Michigan, so we know what real weather is.

The game starts and the wind is really blowing out to left. Both teams play well and the game is pretty tight through the 4th inning. Then, the rain came and our pitchers could no longer find the strike zone. It showered on and off for about 30 minutes and the 70 degree weather now felt like 50 with the wet stuff coming down and the wind still blowing. The game ends after five innings. After a quick pep talk, we all go home. The heater never felt so good in my Ford. All I could think about was a hot shower and a warm bed.

I arrive home to find Connor on my side of the bed. He looks very comfortable, so I leave him alone. I thaw out in the shower and spend a little time in the office doing some work. I am feeling pretty strong and I notice that the middle and end of the day is not nearly as hard as the beginning. I realize that when I wake up, I have some work to do because of all the rain. The chance of our games being cancelled tomorrow is very likely. Our league has four teams in it, and 3 games are on the schedule for Saturday morning & afternoon. That means as the league administrator, I have to go out, assess the field, and then contact 48 families as early as possible to tell them if they have a game or not. Sometimes being the boss really stinks, but I am blessed to be able to get paid coaching baseball.

I go in the bedroom to go to sleep, but realize I have not read the bible yet tonight and when I don't my mind is a complete mess. It acts like a cleanser for me. My former pastor used to combat people who told him that Christians are brainwashed. He said you're right, the Word of God cleanses your mind and I bet you could use a good brain wash. One of the things I loved about the Pastor Troy's sermons was that they were smart and funny. I sit down on the floor near the bathroom and crack the door so I have enough light to read. I don't want to disturb Taleen and Connor. I go to one of my favorite places in the bible, Psalm 112. I call this the blueprint for how a man should want to model his life. I have such a strong desire to provide for my family and I want this job so bad. All I can do is believe in what I can't see.

AFTERWORD

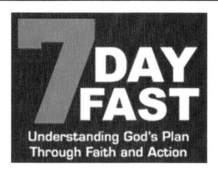

Soreness normally causes physical pain and distress. This morning my soreness appears to be more emotional. Being tired, hungry, and impatient is no way to start one's day but I did make the best of it. As I worked my way through day four, I was determined to get the most out of what turned out to be a long day. Once again, my determination allowed me to be the dad, husband and coach that day four demanded.

Biblical Points to Consider
While Seeking to Understand God's Plan

Sore: Exodus 15:2

Impatient: James 1:12

Determined: 1 Corinthians 9:27

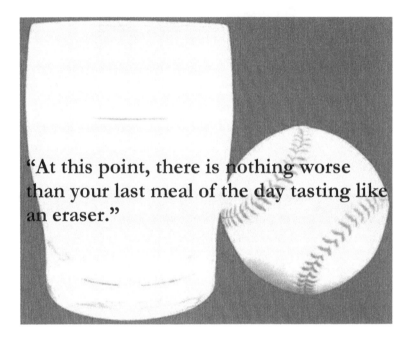

"At this point, there is nothing worse than your last meal of the day tasting like an eraser."

DAY FIVE

AT 5AM I HEAR BRYCE give out a little cry in the baby monitor. I wait for a second to see if he stands up, and when he rolls back over I am praising the name of Jesus because I get to go back to sleep. He lasts another 45 minutes and my day begins. My body could really have used another hour or two, but that's not going to happen. The dogs are ready to go out so I have to bundle up Bryce and take them in the front yard again. It's cold and damp out and Harley is taking her sweet time. This is not happening. I give her a yank on her leash and the 4 of us scurry back in to the 76 degree living room. Connor greets us in the hallway and the party is about to start. No easing into this day.

Thankfully Taleen wakes up around 6, and after we watch the weather channel and get something warm to drink, I go into the office to look up an email I received late yesterday afternoon. The city of Phoenix warned us about the rain and gave us an inclement weather line phone number to call in case the wet stuff hit. I call it up and thank God the recording says all the fields are closed. Now all I have to do is send a mass email to the parents & coaches instead of going to the field and checking it out myself. However, my work is unfortunately not done.

Our regular season was supposed to end today, with playoffs starting next week. The rainouts throw a wrench into everything and to top it off, two of my head coaches are unable to attend any games past November 16th. Two of our teams still need to play at least one more regular season game to even out the league standings, so our double elimination playoff tournament now goes to single elimination. I am not a fan of this, but it makes the most sense. I go online, update the schedule and email everyone again with the new info.

The boys are on fire this morning and Taleen is having a very hard time with them. Her patience is thin and I can tell that not hearing from the Giants is starting to wear on her. She is very concerned about our finances and the boys throwing blocks across the room into the wall is not helping. My head is banging from hunger pains and the boy's disobedience is getting on my nerves. I am ready to spank them both, so I know we all need a change of scenery.

It's now around 9:30am and Bryce needs a nap. I take both boys in the car to give T a break and to get BroHo to count some sheep. I have some errands to run, so we stop at the bank to deposit some cash and then go fill up the gas tank. Taleen and I need to leave the house again at 10:30am to go over and speak at a church meeting. So, I pull both boys back inside and jump into some respectable clothes that she hand picks. Thankfully, Bryce is still conked out in his car seat. So, we get in and out pretty quickly. Now, it's off to Impact Church to speak to a group of single women.

48

Taleen and I get to the church and pull out a bunch of toys for the boys to play with. We share the story of how we met and how waiting for a Godly man is more important than settling for a guy who seems to fit the bill. The boys are getting antsy. After being at church for almost 2 hours, they need some lunch. Connor also needs to go to sleep. He is being very defiant today and has told us no about 25 times. It's going on 1pm, I am not dealing well with his yelling and I am getting hungry. Taleen sees my frustration and drops me off at the house in hopes that the boys will calm down in the car after a ride.

I get in the house and the silence is so serene. I go above the stove to grab the Magic Bullet, but before I can even blend my chocolaty peanutbuttery goodness, I get a call from Taleen. Connor has decided to pee in his car seat because he is upset. She is furious and when they come home the chaos sets in. I end up having to grab the paddle (spare the rod, spoil the child) and tan Connor's butt with a couple of swats. He falls asleep on the couch with a bottle of milk and it's one down, one to go.

Bryce is showing us no signs of being tired. So, we play with him on the floor with some balls and discuss the minor league coaching job situation. What scares Taleen the most is if none of the 30 teams offer us a job, what do we do next? Our baseball business is obviously not cutting it and I have no idea what else I am going to do. I've worked in offices and I have taught before, but never liked any of my jobs outside of coaching. I tell Taleen it's like being 6'5", 315 pounds and deciding to try out for wide receiver. It makes no sense. You go where your strengths are and I firmly believe that I am in the right profession to not only provide for my family, but also further God's kingdom by sharing my faith in an arena where there are not always a lot of Christians. We end our discussion by praying to God and claiming the Giants job as our own. We don't know when it's going to happen, but His timing is always perfect.

T and I desperately need some time to just hang out alone and the only way to do it is for Bryce to take a nap. She leaves the house with Bryce and tells me to jump in bed and relax until she gets home. The kitchen is a war zone, so instead I decide to clean it up and then go in the office and get in the Word. She gets home as I am finishing up the final chapter in the book of Daniel and we go in our bedroom to discuss it. Finally, we have some time to ourselves and we cuddle up, talk and watch the Food Channel on the tube. I may not be able to eat any of it, but I am getting some good ideas on how I want to break my fast on Monday night. Seafood gumbo and jambalaya is sounding really good right about now.

The phone rings and its Mike, the guy who does our league uniforms. We have a big baseball clinic out at Chase Field tomorrow and I ordered some new shirts for our coaches. He did a rush job for me so we need to meet up this afternoon. His shop is about 30 miles away, but luckily he is driving my way and agrees to meet me at a restaurant nearby. Taleen wants a cheese pizza for dinner so I figure I can pick up both of these items at the same time.

The boys wake up as I am about to leave and Connor wants to tag along. We take Bo with us and go meet up with Mike. I leave both of them in the truck as I run in to grab the pizza. On our way home, Connor wants to eat some now because he slept through lunch. He has another meltdown when I tell him he has to wait and the fireworks start again. We get home and after a few minutes Taleen and the boys sit down to eat. I need to pack the truck with all the baseball equipment for tomorrow. So, I sneak out the back door because if Connor sees me, he will immediately leave the dinner table to see what I am up to. Luckily I am in Black Ops mode and get my work done without interruption.

All I want is my fruit flavored shake for dinner, but when I come back inside, Taleen had just finished bathing Bryce which meant I need to do the same for Connor. I am feeling tired and weak, but after about 20 minutes, we are done and no bombs went off. I sit down on the floor and this time the shake is chalky. At this point, there is nothing worse than your last meal of the day tasting like an eraser. So, I need something else. I go warm up some milk, sprinkle in some cinnamon and add a little vanilla creamer. This goes down smooth and I am feeling really good.

A shower is my next goal. I am excited to get in, but then Bryce and Connor get into a fight over the dump truck. Taleen is near tears and I end up going in the bathroom, kneel down and pray that the boys would behave and that Taleen would be able to rest. Connor comes into our bedroom and lies down on the bed. Bryce calms down so I am in the clear. Thank you, Lord. I have not shaved since Wednesday so I am overdue. I am able to get about 20 minutes of peace as I get cleaned up and then the boys are at it again. Taleen is a wreck and I have to help her out. It's back to the living room to try and settle this night down.

Bryce is rolling around and he just needs to go to bed. Taleen takes him in for his final bottle of the night and Connor and I say prayers on the couch. He crashes there and once Taleen comes out of the bedroom with a thumbs up, I carry Bryce into his room and place him in the crib. T and I get another opportunity to hang out and this time the Food Network is making me really hungry. The host of the show keeps "rolling out" to all these cool places to eat and the food is killing me. I am physically hungry.

Taleen falls asleep at 9pm and I head back into the office to chronicle the day's events. I stay up until 11:30 pm writing and I am praying that the boys sleep through the night. Going to bed this late is stupid because they are getting up by 6am no matter what. Maybe Taleen will let me sleep in. We shall see.

I get in the Word before I go down to bed. It's been a hard day. So, I go to two of my favorite scriptures which are both found in Romans. In Romans 5: 1-5, it talks about peace, joy, perseverance in difficult times, character and hope. A definite go to. I then travel a few pages to my right and read Romans 12: 1-8. This discusses not conforming to the ways of the world and that we have all been given special talents from the Lord. It is our job to use these talents to bring glory to His name. This encourages me and I know that I am supposed to be teaching baseball. All I need now is the money to provide for my family while I am doing it. Please move on our behalf Lord.

AFTERWORD

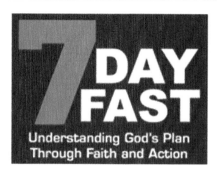

Uncertainty has a way of shaking the best of us. The fear around not being selected by any of the 30 teams was beginning to affect Taleen and myself. However, I knew that similar to how one's body fears hunger and stores any morsel of nutriment as fat, I too must be prepared for "rainy days". It was only day five and there was still the need to keep the faith. As a matter of fact, even with the temptation brought on by watching the "Food Network", I still felt filled with my faith.

Biblical Points to Consider
While Seeking to Understand God's Plan

Fearful: Psalm 112:7

Hungry: Job 23:12

Faith Filled: Hebrews 11:1

"During long drives I use the time to pray and I spend time thinking about the fast. It's starting to wind down and in about 30 hours I will be eating dinner for the first time in a week with my family."

DAY SIX

BRYCE SLEEPS UNTIL 5:30AM and Taleen takes care of him. She is awesome. I get out of bed, make her some coffee and take the mutts out for a bathroom break because they think everyone is up for the morning. No shot. Taleen knows I am beat down, so she tells me to go back to sleep and that she'll come get me at 7am. Connor wakes up as I crawl back into bed and proceeds to open and close our bedroom door over and over. I keep getting flashes of light in the room and nicely ask him to close the door and go play. He does so and I am encouraged that everything will go smooth this morning.

At 6:45am I get hit in the face with a blinding light from above. No, it's not Jesus on the road to Damascus, just the light fixture above our bed. Taleen has turned it on and all I hear now is yelling from her and the two boys. My quiet bedroom has now turned into Grand Central Station. The only residents of our home not making a ruckus are the dogs. Connor and Bryce are not obeying and Taleen is fed up. She needs me to feed them now so she can jump in the shower and get ready for church. She has to be there by 8am since she is on staff and I can tell she just wants to be alone. I ask for a minute to get my bearings and then roll out of the rack and tend to breakfast.

Bryce starts out with some multi-grain Cheerios and Connor wants cold pizza. I feed the dogs their kibble and sprinkle some cheese on top for a little sustenance. Connor sees this and wants some of the cheese, but I let him know he has some on his pizza and when he finishes that, he can have some of the shredded cheese. That is not the answer he was looking for, so after 2 bites he tells me he's done so he can move on to something else. I let him know that we can't waste food and when he gets out of his chair with his plate I warn him to not throw it away.

Well, you can guess what happens. Into the trash can it goes and he laughs. I make the decision to go old school like my parents and he is done eating for the morning. I break out some peaches for Bryce and even though Connor pleads for some, he has to stay in his chair and watch his brother eat. We finish breakfast with yogurt chips and Connor is not happy. I ignore his rants and move on to washing dishes. He continues to misbehave and my blood is starting to boil, so I begin to pray. As Taleen leaves the house, the boys start to settle in and play together.

After church today, I have two big baseball clinics at Chase Field. I go into the bedroom to get ready and as I am packing my bag Connor sees my mitt. He wants to play catch and how can I resist. The glove is only 11 inches, but is big and clunky for him. He decides he wants to throw to me so we grab a rubber baseball and he fires about 20 pitches across the living room. He has a great arm and his accuracy is pretty good too. He steps with the wrong foot, but heck, the kid is only three. We finish up by putting the glove on him and doing some short distance catch. He gets the hang of it. When I tell him it's time to go to church, he is compliant and the morning all the sudden went from the outhouse to the penthouse.

We get to church late and since Connor is still not feeling up to snuff, we only check Bryce into the childcare. Connor and I decide to stay in the church foyer and listen to the service on the TV monitor. Connor wolfs down a donut and Taleen comes out of the sanctuary to take over. Five of my coaches go to our church and all of them have played with the Los Angeles Angels. They want to go to lunch before we head down to the ballpark. We decide to go to Wildflower Café. I had made a chocolate/peanut butter shake before I left the house and put it in the fridge at church. So, I grabbed that and drank it on my way. I am not sharing the news of the fast with anyone, because I don't want to draw attention to myself. Not eating will not be a big deal, because I can just tell them I had a late breakfast and I'm not hungry.

I get to Wildflower and they have already ordered. I sit down and one of the guys isn't eating either, so the subject doesn't even come up. We discuss the concert they went to last night and the new front office employee the Angels just hired. This person will be very influential in which minor league coaches they hire. I have already traded emails the current Manager of Baseball Operations with the Angels, and after talking more with the guys, I consider giving him a call this week. Maybe the Giants won't come through after all and the Angels will be our future employer. I don't know, but I am going to do whatever I can to provide for this family.

Everyone finishes up and we head to Chase Field. I am encouraged by the news that the Angels are beginning to hire

57

front office employees, because I know once that starts happening, hiring coaches will not be too far down the road.
The Angels had re-assigned or let go of at least 4 high profile employees and putting those people in place starts the process for someone like me to get interviews. I call Taleen to let her know and look forward to the clinics at Chase. It's going to be awesome to be on a big league field and have so much room to work with. The 10 coaches I have hired to help me are top notch and we all have a great time together. I miss the camaraderie that playing the game brings, so being around all of these guys is awesome.

During long drives, I use the time to pray and I spend time thinking about the fast. It's starting to wind down and in about 30 hours I will be eating dinner for the first time in a week with my family. Taleen has told me on multiple occasions that the first day of the fast is always the hardest for her and that it gets a little easier as the days go by. I never believed her, but I have noticed after I got through the fourth day I was not craving food as much and that my body seems to be adjusting to the regimen of liquid only. I also realized that my prayer time has not been as powerful the past couple of days. I tend to pray harder, the more difficult time I am going through. That's when it hits me --- a fast without prayer is simply a diet.

One of my good friends and one of the men who stood next to me the day I married Taleen is Pastor Scott. He knows scripture better than anyone I have ever met and he once wrote on his Facebook page that "God is not a genie". He was referring to people who fast, but they don't get deeper into prayer. They are giving up something they desire, usually food, but they are not using the time to get closer to God. That really resonated with me at this time and I dedicated myself to pray more for the next day and a half.

We arrive at Chase around noon and put all of the baseball equipment on a flat cart so that it can be taken to the field. All of the coaches meet in the visitor's clubhouse on the first base side and catch up on each other's lives as we watch a little football. Drew Beuerlein is one of my coaches and he has become a very good friend even though we have only known each other for a year. I have started to rely on him a lot in the business so it goes to show you that quality outweighs quantity almost every time. Drew & I head out to the field to assess the area and I go over my game plan with him on where I envision the different stations that the players will be running through. We head back in the clubhouse, go over the plan with the coaches and it's time to shine!

The Kiwanis Club is putting this event on and they were unsure of how many registrations they would have. During our meetings we agreed to cap the number at 150 players. I made preparations for that number, but in my mind also had back up plans for a lower amount. The first clinic has 72 players in it, so we decide to trim the number of stations from 10 to 8 and we start right on time at 1:30pm. I float for most of the 2 hours in-between stations, making sure they rotate on time and that the coaches are doing good. In order to keep the guys fresh I have them run different stations every 2 or 3 rotations so they don't get bored doing the same thing 8 times in a row. I end up throwing batting practice during the 8th station and we finish 10 minutes early. Just in time to give the players a talk and give my coaches a breather. They head into the clubhouse and grab something to eat. The next clinic is set to begin at 3:30pm.

After I dismiss the first group, I go over and I am told by a Kiwanis member that we have 120 players for the second clinic. Gulp. That's almost twice as many as the first. So, I walk over to the security guard who is monitoring the second group of players and let him know we will be starting 10 minutes late.

I want to let the coaches know about the larger group and go over a new game plan. I'm not really that nervous because 4 years ago I did a Little League clinic up in Cave Creek and we had 150 kids on a little league field which is half as large as Chase Field. We ended up marching 60 of them over to a soccer field to make it work, but in the end we put on a good clinic that day.

I head back into the clubhouse to break the news and some of the guys get saucer-eyed at the number. We go back to our original 10 station plan and I tell them to finish eating and come on out in a couple of minutes. I bring the new group of kids out on the field and the number they told was way off. We have a max of 85 players and immediately we go back to our 8 station plan. This clinic goes smooth as well and again we finish on time. The Kiwanis members are beaming at the job we did and are already discussing how they want to do it again next year. I didn't get paid today, but my coaches did and trust me, this was an investment for the future. We all had fun and now it's time to go home.

I told Taleen that I would be home no later than 7pm and after changing out of my uniform and packing up, I am in the truck by 6. I call her up to hear about her day and let her know that I will be home in 30 minutes. She had a difficult time with Connor, but she was able to get her work done when both boys went down for a late nap. The CoHo is still asleep on the couch when I get home, but wakes up soon after. Taleen and Bryce had already eaten so I make my way into the kitchen to make my fruit flavored smoothie for dinner. This one tastes better than last night, but I flash back to the goodness that was the warm milk I had afterwards and repeat the mixture again this evening. It was just as tasty as the night before and I am feeling pretty good. This time tomorrow I will be eating solid food again. Connor grubs some lasagna and due to the fact that he napped late, he is not going to bed at his normal 8pm time.

BroHo fell asleep in our room with Taleen and I carry him into his crib. I kneel down and pray for both boys and by the time I finish, Connor is in his pajamas and has crawled into bed with Taleen. The three of us stay up and watch Food Network. My jaws start to hurt while watching. Taleen laughs at me in a sympathetic way and we discuss what we will be having for dinner tomorrow. I won't be home until 6:30pm from doing lessons, so I wanted to keep it simple for her. I decide on salmon, asparagus and wild rice. It's a pretty easy make for her with not much prep time necessary. Just the oven and a stove top and she is set. The boys will be all over her most likely so making a large dish like gumbo or jambalaya is a bad idea.

Connor falls asleep and by 9pm Taleen is ready too. I am going to learn my lesson from last night and turn in as well, but before I do, I gotta get in the Word. I go over to the light that is illuminated by the bathroom and sit on the floor with my back to the wall. I read Psalm 27 which is an exuberant declaration of faith. I have to believe that this job is mine! It's so hard when you don't get the phone calls for at least an interview, but I have to stay positive and believe that if it's not the Giants then there is something else out there that is going to bless us more!

Tomorrow morning may not be as easy with Bryce-man. I am expecting some fireworks because it's the final day of the fast and I am convinced the devil will be coming out guns blaring, trying to steal my victory. I am not going to let that happen. Connor is feeling better and coughing less so I take him into his bed. I don't think he will wake up Bryce. I let the dogs out one last time, pray to clear my mind and hit the hay. Tomorrow I eat!

AFTERWORD

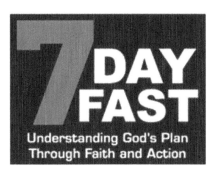

For some strange reason, day six seemed to bring excitement and optimism. Even though there was no call yet from the Giants for an interview, I still feel that a baseball job will soon be mine. It was encouraging to hear how the Angels were shaking up things. With change comes opportunity for someone. It's hard not to anticipate that very soon the phone will ring and something will surely come my way.

Biblical Points to Consider
While Seeking to Understand God's Plan

Excited: Jeremiah 29:11

Enlightened: Ephesians 1:18

Anticipation: Joshua 1:9

"I feel good about the Angels and wonder if that's who I am supposed to be with. Maybe that's why the Giants haven't called yet."

DAY SEVEN

IT'S ALL QUIET IN THE HOME until around 2am. Bryce is sounding off, but we wait and he falls back to sleep within a minute. This happens again an hour later with the same result. Now, Connor leaves their room and crawls into bed with us. At 5:15am Connor is awake and wants everyone else to join him. For the next 45 minutes he flips around in bed and it's not the way I wanted to start the morning. At 6am Bryce wakes up and we all roll out of bed together. Connor is elated.

I go into the bathroom to weigh myself. I started the fast at 194 and I feel most comfortable in my own skin when I am around 200 so I felt light from the beginning. When I played I would get up to 215 in the offseason and then maintain somewhere in the low 200 range. I step on the scale this morning and I am 182. I lost a lot of weight early in the fast, but have maintained the past couple of days. I have not been this light since I was 17 as a high school senior. That was half my life ago. I feel skinny and when I look in the mirror I can see it. Oh, well. For a while I used to work so hard on

65

taking care of my body and neglected my soul. I needed to go through this fast for so many reasons and it is worth it.

I take the dogs out front, Taleen curls up on the couch with her coffee and the boys play together on the floor. Things are going well until Connor defiantly disobeys Taleen multiple times in a row. He is sitting on top of a plastic bulldozer and he won't get off. She's afraid he is going to break it or fall off, but he won't listen. She removes him, he goes back. She takes it away. He runs and gets it. This goes on for a minute and finally he yells "NO" at her. I step in, give him a swat on the butt for talking to Mommy that way and put him in time out. Oh Lord, help me be patient.

At this point of the fast, I am tired and I just want some peace and quiet. That is not going to happen when you are a husband and father, so I dig in deep and push through the morning. Today is a school day for Connor and I am taking him today. Taleen needs to be at work by 9am and the church is providing a babysitter for Bryce. All I need to do is take him to the playground, hang out for a few minutes and then the solace I desire will be mine. It's still cool out, so I am in no rush to get there. By the time I arrive the kids are already in the classroom and school begins in 5 minutes. Perfect. I put his lunch in the fridge, give him a hug and pass him on to his teacher, Ms. Tracy.

On the drive home, I start thinking about the Angels. I am going to call them today and hopefully I will get to talk to someone, instead of just communicating via email. I want to get a pulse on what is going on and it's easier to do so over the phone. Emails have no emotion and it can be hard to read the person on the other side. I also want to contact the Rangers, because their old Farm Director is the man that the Angels just hired over the weekend. All of my communication with the

Rangers was emails I sent to him, so I want to contact his old assistant just in case that guy gets the job. Rumor is they will be promoting from within and I think he may be the guy who gets it. If not, I am hoping he will pass my resume on to the person who they hire.

I get home and get in the Word. Taleen and I have started to study the prophet Elijah. It is truly amazing all of the things that the Lord does through him and much like Daniel, he gives God all the glory. Elijah is humble and reliant upon God for provision from the beginning as we learn in 1 Kings 17:2-6 when the Lord provides him bread and meat delivered by ravens. That my friend, is trusting the Lord. I start to pray and now understand that I need to make sure that I give God all the glory during this fast. He is the one who has given me the strength, endurance and determination to get through this. He has inspired me to write this book which I believe will help others. I get off my knees, thank Him again and get to work.

It's time to call the Angels. I am excited to talk to someone, but all I get is a recording. They are an hour behind us so I have to wait until 10am to get a live person in the office. I don't like leaving messages because I never know if the person is going to get it. I move on to the Rangers and get a voicemail for the person I am trying to reach over there in the player development department. I decide to send him an email discussing my interest in a minor league coaching position and include the communication that I have had with the organization so far. Their spring training facility is in Surprise, Arizona which is about an hour with traffic from us, but only 5 minutes from my Mom's house. I caught in the bullpen for them 8 years ago during Spring Training and their organization is top notch right now.

It's not time to call the Angels yet. So, I move on to my work with Cactus Athletic Camps, returning emails and checking league registrations. We had a lot of people sign up over the weekend which is encouraging. I also set up my lessons for the week and I have 8 so far. Not bad considering it's only Monday. I get on my knees and thank the Lord for his provision. It's not the job I am seeking, but the business is growing and all money is green no matter how you earn it. I gotta earn some bread so I can put some on the table.

I work through the 10 o'clock hour and give their manager of Baseball Operations a call at 10:30am. He picks up his line and we have a very nice 5 minute conversation. I let him know my interest and that I am impressed with the high level of character that his players possess. I am also friends with one of the pitching coaches for the Angels in rookie ball as well. He thanks me and says that they will probably be making some coaching decisions in a couple of weeks.

I feel good about the Angels and wonder if that's who I am supposed to be with. Maybe that's why the Giants haven't called yet. I'm not sure but I know I need to give my family more stability and I want to work in pro ball. The other team that I am pretty certain that there are some openings with, are the Padres. I make a phone call to their Farm Director and leave him a message. I don't think he is ever in the office, but I am told that he does check voicemails. I have actually met him a couple of times in the past and one of my good friends, Kory, who is now with the Pirates, put in a good word for me last month. Kory was a hitting coach in the Midwest League for the Padres this past season and was offered a better job by the Pirates about a month ago. He left the Padres on good terms and his word is good in the baseball world. Someone call me please!

My first lesson today is at 2pm out at Scottsdale Ranch Park with Adam, the left handed pitcher I met with last Wednesday. It's been raining out off and on this weekend so I shoot him a text at 11am and ask him to check out the mound after he gets out of school to see if we can use it. Adam has early release and is done before noon. He also lives across the street from the park so it's not a big deal for him to go investigate for me. He is a really great kid and I want to do a good job to help him get to where he wants to be as a pitcher.

I sift through some new emails and around 11:30am Taleen calls and asks me to pick up Connor from school. She is hung up at work and can't break free. Not a big deal. My mind is thinking about how much I want dinner tonight, so nothing is gonna bring me down. Before I leave to pick him up, I contemplate making a shake to drink. This morning I considered not having any shakes today and just going straight water like the normal fast I do. I really wanted the Lord to stretch me today and I feel like I pray better and harder when I'm hungry. Drinking that shake would satisfy my hunger and all I have had to drink up to this point today is H2O. Done, I've made up my mind. Water it is, and I am excited for what God has for me.

As I take off in the truck on my way to get CoHo, Adam lets me know that the mound is not good to throw off of. It's soft and there is a puddle near the bottom of it. We decide to meet tomorrow and Thursday instead, which I am happy about. Now, all I have is a 4pm & 5pm lesson at an indoor facility. This will be easier on my body and I will still be able to meet with Adam this week. It also confirms with me that going straight water today was the right decision. One of the reasons I considered not doing it was for strength purposes, but I told God my strength comes from Him so I would be fine. Like it says in Phil 4:13, "I can do all things in Christ who strengthens me."

Connor is excited to see me, but not really willing to leave school right away. I bribe him with going to watch the "horsies", and he follows me off the playground. Actually getting him in the truck is a different story and he becomes very disobedient to the point where I have to chase him down on the outskirts of the parking lot. This really irks me, so I tell him that he has lost his privilege to see the horses and I ignore him on the drive home. He begins to yell at me. So, now I make the decision to stick him in time out for a while as well.

We get home and he is on fire. Normally, when I put him in time out he goes in the corner of his room, sits down for 2 minutes, and I call him back out. His door is open during this and the lights are on. This time I close the door and hold it shut on the other side while I am sitting on the ground. It's an awful incident, as he is yelling and crying while hanging on the doorknob in the room. All I want is for him to be obedient so we can hang out. Disciplining him is my least favorite thing to do, but I know I have to for his own good. That is one of the major reasons I am fasting this week. I want the Lord to reveal to me things I need to work on to be a better dad, which will also turn me into a better husband.

Connor lets up after a few minutes and we have a little talk. I tell him how much I love him and that he needs to learn to obey his parents. He's only three, but I believe I am making a dent so I try to always talk to him like I would someone who is older. I do not do baby talk and I don't lie to my son. A little white lie is still a big fat stinking lie in my book. I am straight up with him, but also only give him information that he needs to know. After all, he is three.

We sit down to eat the lunch he didn't finish at school and he does not seem interested. He has graham crackers and a partially eaten peanut butter and honey sandwich. I get the idea to make his sandwich crunchy by putting the graham cracker inside of it. That's what I do sometimes. He likes it and before you know it, his plate is clean. The next time I sit at this table I will be eating with him. Taleen calls me again and this time I need to come to church to pick up Bryce. I figure at this time of the day both boys will fall asleep on the way home which will give me some quiet time before my lessons.

On my way to church I get a phone call from one of my mentors, Bill Crawford. He is an awesome man of God and lives in Battle Creek, Michigan. He was there for me during a very rough part of my life six years ago. I frequently go to him for advice and prayer. I had called him a few days back because I wanted him to pray for the Giants job. During our conversation he tells me that I need to write down everything I am going through for the next 10 to 14 days because he feels like it will help others as well. This brings a big smile to my face and I decide to tell him about the fast and the notes I have been already writing. Up to this point the only person who knows about it is Taleen. In Matthew 6:16-18, Jesus teaches about fasting and that we should not let everyone know we are doing it. That would be glorifying us and not God. Bill lets me know that what I told him confirms what the Lord put on his heart and when I pull into the church parking lot he prays for me. He is so awesome and I love that man so much. I have not seen him since I moved back to Arizona in 2006 and I miss him a lot. Hopefully, we will meet up again soon.

Taleen meets me at the door and we put Bryce into the truck hassle free. We get a minute to talk about our day and I share with her about my decision to go water only today. You can tell that she is really proud of me because she knows my intentions are pure. I want to be a better man for her and I know the Lord is going to bless us. The boys and I go by the horse properties and Bryce falls asleep. Connor is not giving in so as we drive home he assures me that he will take a nap on the couch. We get home and I pop in a penguin cartoon video for CoHo. I make some coffee for T because she is struggling with energy today and I take a little time to do some writing in the office.

Around 3pm Taleen gets home and I shut down my work to spend a little time with her. Connor is still awake, but at least the penguins are keeping him occupied. I get a text from my friend Derin who will be the Rookie Ball Manager next year with the Giants. He lets me know that he just got his contract signed and that the reason I have probably not heard anything yet, is that they are going through the process of taking care of their current coaches right now. We message back and forth a little and by the end of it I am very encouraged. Even though I would take a job from someone else if they offered it, I really want to coach with Derin in Rookie Ball next year. I want to be a Giant.

I jump into the truck at 3:30pm and make my way over to Inside Pitch to do my lessons. All of the sudden I get this burst of energy. It's the strongest I have felt during the fast. I start praising God and decide that it's time to do some serious praying. I lay out all the reasons why I want this job and make sure that all my motives and reasons are pure. I feel like as I am looking through the windshield everything is more vibrant and colorful as if I went from watching a normal TV to one in high definition. I pop on the stereo and after one song finishes, "Courageous" by Casting Crowns comes over the airwaves. My eyes well up and I almost start crying. This confirms the improvement in fatherhood that I have been praying for during this fast. Taleen and I went and saw this movie the night we broke her 3 day fast and we walked out of the theatre knowing we wanted to be better parents. I am flying to work now and my spirit is soaring!

I get to the indoor facility and my first lesson is early. He is already in a batting cage taking some hacks off the machine. His name is Tyler and he is a stout 9 year old. The kid is pretty strong and has a nice swing. We have been doing pitching lessons for the past 2 months and this is our seventh session. He wants to learn how to throw 6 pitches for strikes including curves and sliders, so I have to pull the throttle back a little on this one. I tell young kids all the time to just throw the ball down the middle and I can show you 3 separate fast balls that will locate in different places by the way you grip the seams. The four seam goes straight, the two seam moves in and the cutter moves away. If they can also master a changeup, which has the same rotation as a fastball, but is about 7-10 miles per hour slower and fades down in the zone, they will be dominant.

Tyler is a fun kid to work with. We talk about his day at school and I always ask him what his favorite part was. Shockingly today it was music class. Normally the answer is always recess or P.E. What do you expect? He's 9! He also plays football and his mom emailed me an interception he made last month. He is a pretty good athlete. I notice my energy is getting sapped towards the end of the hour when he is throwing his bullpen. I only have one lesson left and I am 90 minutes away from eating salmon with my family. My next client is 15 minutes early and starts doing some warm up drills outside the cage. I dismiss Tyler and I look forward to seeing him in two weeks.

It's time for Desmond to make an appearance. He has played in our league, attended our camps and has done private lessons over the past 4 years. This is our 34th private lesson. He is on the smaller side and is pretty quiet, but a super kid, who never complains about his playing time or coaches. He has wanted to focus on pitching lately so we work on that for 30 minutes and then finish up with hitting. The funny thing about Des is that he has trouble locating during drills, but in his bullpen sessions he throws a lot of strikes. They are not very fast, but he gets them over the dish. His energy level is pretty low and the lesson is not going great. His hitting has improved a lot this year, but tonight it is sub-par. We talk at the end and I let him know that he is much better than what he showed tonight. I will see him at practice on Wednesday and we will meet again next Monday.

Bump, bump, bum! One more hurdle to the finish line. I just have to get home safe and dinner is only 30 minutes away! I say goodbye to the people at the front desk and jump in the truck. I give Taleen a call and after a couple of minutes she needs to tend to Bryce so she thinks this will be a good time for me to pray on my way home. What an awesome wife! It starts to rain and my mind wanders back to an awful car wreck I was involved in 8 years ago around this time. I know the devil has been attacking me throughout the day, but my God is more powerful than him so I dismiss any negative thoughts and focus on the road. I send out a prayer of thanksgiving again to the Lord and cruise into the driveway unharmed. I am so glad that I did not drink that shake today. The Lord provided me with all the strength I needed. Now, it's time to eat!

The dogs meet me at the door and the boys are already sitting down at the table. My lovely wife has taken care of everything and asks me to sit down. This meal as she states it is all about me. The salmon and asparagus are cooked perfectly. The center of the fish is moist and juicy and the asparagus has a nice crack to it. She also has some homemade babaganoosh that was left over from a couple of days ago and I eat that with pita chips. My wife's parents are Armenian and she is an awesome cook. I especially love it when I get the opportunity to eat the food that she grew up on. My stomach starts to hurt a little and even though I am hungry for more I decide to stop while I'm ahead. I still need some dessert and unfortunately we don't have enough of what I want.

I was craving a certain cereal on my way home and I knew we were running low on it. It's a chocolate hazelnut biscotti granola made by Archer Farms. I can only find it at Target and there is one on my way back from Inside Pitch, but Taleen emphasized that she wanted me home pronto. I use what is left in the cupboard, which is miniscule. I add Grape Nuts and Cocoa Puffs to it, which is a mistake. I am not feeling it. Oh well, dinner was great and I am not going to focus on this. Connor sits down next to me with some Cocoa Puffs in a bowl and we hang out the couch watching TV. We do this a lot and it's some good bonding time before bed.

My stomach starts to grumble and I have to make it to the bathroom pretty quick. I have only pooped twice during the fast. The first time was on Wednesday and everything was regular. Earlier today I went and it was more solid than I expected. I actually felt a little constipated which shocked me because all I had was liquids for a week. This is a little diarrhea and now I am concerned I might be on the pot all night long. Oh well, this was still worth it.

The process is quick and I am back in the family room with everyone. The night goes by pretty good and Connor falls asleep on the couch before Bryce goes down. I always put Connor to bed and Taleen always takes care of Bryce. She smirks at me and comments on how I have it easy tonight. All I can think of is, "It's the Lord's favor, baby"! I leave the

Monday Night Football game on for some background noise and walk into the office to get some writing done. The office has French doors that swing open to the living room so I can check on Connor and the game at the same time. I work until 10:30pm and then get in the Word. Tonight, I go to Psalm 28 which talks about rejoicing in answered prayer. I am believing in the Giants job even though I don't have it yet. Walking out my faith!!!

AFTERWORD

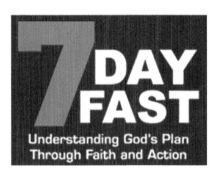

As day seven unfolded, I realized that I was about 30 pounds below my baseball playing weight and was beginning to feel "skinny". However, the day would get much better. I was thankful that I have made it through the fast to this point without any physical incidents. Today, I am actually feeling energized for having walked out my faith.

Biblical Points to Consider
While Seeking to Understand God's Plan

Skinny: 1 Corinthians 19,20

Thankful: Isaiah 26:3,4

Energized: Ephesians 3:16

"The phone rings about a quarter to 9 and it's him. He beat me to the punch and right away I double check the clock to make sure I wasn't late in calling him."

AFTER THE FAST

TUESDAY MORNING HITS and the fast is over. It's back to a normal diet routine now and I really want to be careful of what I am consuming. I realized during the fast that my sugar intake was too high and even though I eat pretty clean, I want to be better. I also make a commitment to be more in prayer throughout the day. Even if it's just a couple of minutes in the truck praying for Taleen and the kids a few times a day, it is a discipline I want to improve. I need to spend less time listening to sports talk on the radio and more time with Jesus.

Over the month of November, I continue to scour the internet for possible information on job openings with any of the teams and I stay in contact with Derin about the Giants opening. His family came over for a barbeque on the 19th and while our wives are inside, our kids are in the backyard playing while we tend to the chicken on the grill. I haven't heard anything about the job and I don't want to bring it up. But, Derin figures it's on my mind so we talk about the possibility of working together and it gets us both excited. His son Katch is 4 years old and is a really good kid. He and Connor are pretty good buds and they push around toy lawnmowers and take some swings off the tee with some whiffle balls. I can already imagine the two of them paling around in the locker room and running in the outfield together at the Giants facility. This job seems so perfect for our family in so many ways. But, so far the phone isn't ringing.

Thanksgiving comes and still no job. It shows me what I truly need to be thankful for and I am so blessed to have my family and the amazing friends that I am surrounded by. About 20 of us meet for dinner over at Andre and Subyn's house and it's nice to just forget about work, watch a little football and swap old stories of when we were younger. I eat way too much, the same thing I do every Thanksgiving, and now I wish I was fasting instead of my gut feeling like it's going to bust. Dessert put me over the edge, but it looked too good to pass up. I go out to the car and get some pineapple & papaya tablets that I keep in the glove box of both vehicles. I get them from Trader Joe's and they help with food digestion. They work quickly and are tasty as well. We hang out with our friends for a little longer and then head home for a much needed family weekend.

Major League Baseball holds its annual winter meetings every year in early December and this year Dallas is the host city. All 30 teams meet for 4 days and a lot of decisions get made during the meetings. Free agents signings, trades and filling in coaching slots are some of the many things that clubs discuss. I figure if I am going to get a job for the 2012 season, something will happen this week. I actually attended the meetings back in 2002 when they were hosted in Anaheim and it was a bit of a circus. Lots of people sit in the lobby with resumes trying to get 5 minutes with team officials with a wide array of motives, mostly trying to find a job. I pray long and hard about going to Dallas, but I just don't feel like it's going to make a difference, so I stay home.

Monday, the 5th is the first day for the winter meetings and the phone doesn't ring. I can't obsess about this, so I just focus on my private lessons and our youth baseball league. In Matthew 6:34 it tells us to not worry about tomorrow and sitting around feeling sorry for myself does no good. Tuesday & Wednesday go by and I get nada. No teams are calling and I know that there are jobs out there. Should I have gone to Dallas? Is there someone sitting in a meeting room right now with one of these teams interviewing for a job that I am qualified for? I can't second guess my decision to stay home now. I have to remember it's in God's hands and I need to refocus on being a good daddy to Connor and Bryce. My daddy up in heaven will take care of me and his plan is better than mine. Like most of us, I just wish I knew what the plan was.

Thursday is the last day of the meetings and I think most of it consists of wrap up sessions so I don't expect a call. The day starts off normal with breakfast, canine craziness and the boys playing on the living room floor. Around 11am my cell phone rings and it's the Director of Player Development for the San Francisco Giants. He said he just stepped out of a meeting and that he received the green light to start an interview process with me for the rookie ball hitting coach position here in Arizona! There really isn't a word to describe what I was feeling at that moment so you can insert your own adjective. He needed to go back into the meeting room. So, we talk for about five minutes and at the end of the conversation he said that I would be receiving at least two or three more phone calls from other people in the organization over the next few days. I remember him saying that if these interviews go well, the process will be very quick. I remain calm on the phone, but on the inside I am absolutely on fire. This is actually happening!

On Friday around 1pm I get a call from the Giant's Coordinator of Instruction for the Minor Leagues. I can tell right off the bat that he is passionate about his job and that hiring the right man is just as important as how much baseball you know. Plenty of guys know how to play it and teach it, but you need to be able to relate that to the players and be a good leader at the same time. We talk for about 10 minutes and it goes really well. Just like the interview I had the day before --- we talk mostly about who I am and a little bit about my baseball background. I believe they wanted to get a feel for what kind of person I am. They can look at my resume and call my references for work history. He lets me know that he feels confident in recommending me for the position and that I will be getting a phone call from the Minor League Hitting Coordinator either today or Monday. I am so freaking excited I can barely see straight!

I don't get a whole lot of time to come down from my high because an hour later I get a phone call. It's the Minor League Hitting Coordinator and this man knows his job. We talk for an hour and while some of it is about my background, most of it is nitty, gritty hitting. I love it. He really impresses me with his knowledge and I am excited about the possibility of working alongside him. I am sweating through my shirt at this point because the whole time I am talking to him on the phone, I am burning a hole in the master bedroom carpet with my continuous pacing. I am so into this conversation that I can't sit down. The dogs are on their beds staring at me wondering what the heck is going on. The interview is very positive and he said that he will endorse me for the job.

I tell Taleen the good news and take off to the cage for a hitting lesson. I am absolutely amped and I find it hard to concentrate on anything but the conversations I had today. I don't expect any calls over the weekend and luckily I have some baseball games to coach to keep my mind occupied. I am very confident at this point, but nothing is done until it's done, if you know what I mean. On Saturday my team splits a doubleheader and Sunday consists of church and family time. I don't know if there is going to be a fourth interview, but I can barely wait to wake up Monday morning to find out what is coming next.

Monday is cold and rainy. This morning I am heading over to an indoor facility called Inside Pitch to help my friend Danny with a new audio pitching app that he is creating for cell phones. My job is to catch a minor league pitcher while Danny charts the locations of the pitches and we have someone taping the audio. We need complete silence to get the pop of the mitt so we have limited lighting on due to the hum that some of ceiling lights give off. It's pretty difficult because I am catching a pitcher who is throwing 90mph in low light with off-speed pitches mixed in as well. I keep telling myself "Just don't break your thumb Horton".

On my way to the facility I get a text from the Giant's Director of Player Development. He tells me to contact Derin and meet up with him at the Giants minor league facility to throw some batting practice to hitters. This is the final test. Throwing BP is huge for a minor league coach because you do it almost every day to hitters. If you can't throw consistent strikes, you aren't much help to the organization. I call Derin once I get to Inside Pitch and we schedule a time to meet in about 2 hours. I finish up my session with Danny and on my way to meet up with Derin, I give Taleen a call. She is really excited and we pray together on the phone. I now turn to my music and I am jamming out to Disciple. They are one of my favorites and next to Skillet they are the best band out there.

I get to the Giants complex 30 minutes early and Derin shows me around. I meet up with 4 hitters down in the cage and after about 100 throws the interview is complete. We spend a little time hanging out in the coach's locker room and Derin lets me know he will call and give a thumbs up on my throwing. He thinks that my next phone call will probably come in the form of a contract offer from the Vice President of Baseball Operations. On the way home I give Taleen a call and we are thanking God for the four great interviews. We can do nothing else and everything is in His hands. Now, we wait.

Tuesday morning comes and I make sure the cell phone is charged. Praying and believing for a phone call today! Taleen is anxious and I am trying to not be. I just need focus on the day and try and not think about the job. Good luck with that. My mom used to have a magnet on our fridge that said something about understanding what we can control and leave the rest up to God. She also had another one that said God grant me patience and do it now! I always think of my Grandma Toupalik when I see that magnet. She was 100%, on fire, red hair, Irish Catholic that would burn a hole through you with her glare when you did something she didn't like. God's timing is always perfect and Tuesday, in His mind was not the perfect day. Ugghhh…

It's Wednesday and all the bars on my iPhone are full. When it rings with a 415 area code I will be prepared. Connor has school this morning. Aside from some baseball lessons tonight, I don't have a whole lot to keep me busy. I continue to tell myself that the job is mine and I look forward to starting next Spring. I relay that to Taleen and she says she would prefer a phone call. It brings us to a conversation on faith and how it is built through adversity. It is believing in something we don't see. It's not tangible. That's what makes it so difficult. It also brings us closer to God. I believe we draw closer to Him through adversity because it gives us a wakeup call. We call out to Him and yearn for His presence in our lives. We need to try and seek Him every day with the fire and passion we have when we are in a difficult situation with our backs against the wall. It shows Him the appreciation and reverence He deserves on a daily basis. As the sun goes behind the mountains here in Scottsdale, we realize the phone will not ring today and our prayer is that it will tomorrow.

The boys get up at 5:30am and Thursday starts early. Breakfast is especially messy. So, Taleen decides to bathe the boys. I am in the kitchen over by the fridge when my phone buzzes. It's a text from the V P of Baseball Ops! It says to give him a call around 9am California time. It's gotta be a contract offer! I sprint though the living room yelling and skid to my knees in the hallway right in front of the open bathroom door. Bryce is in the tub, Connor is standing by and Taleen is elbows deep in suds. Taleen starts crying, and both boys are yelling. They're not sure what they are yelling about, but they just know their parents are being loud and this green lights them to make some obnoxious noise without repercussions. We start praying a prayer of thanksgiving to God out loud and afterwards, Connor and I start dancing like fools. It's a little after 7am, and I can't wait to make this call.

The phone rings about a quarter to 9 and it's him. He beat me to the punch and right away I double check the clock to make sure I wasn't late in calling him. He lets me know about the job and makes the official offer to be a hitting coach for the rookie ball team. We stay on the phone for a few minutes and the whole time I have a smile from ear to ear. He lets me know that a contract will be in the mail soon and that he would like me to start coming down to the Minor League Complex in early January to throw batting practice and catch some bullpens with the early work and rehab players. Shoot, the earlier the better. There is no way I could wait until Spring Training started in March. Get me down there tomorrow!

The day flies by and I make a bunch of phone calls to family, friends and the men who interviewed me. The first call is to my father-in-law, Mo. He has been so generous and helpful over the past 4 years and I want so badly to be able to provide a wonderful life for his daughter. He is very excited and we look forward to seeing each other at Christmas. I call my Mom next and she loses it. She's not really one who cries, so her excited yells are music to my ears and I can hear how proud she is. It's been a long journey with my baseball career and she has stood by me every step of the way. I look forward to her coming out to games next summer.

EPILOGUE

THE JOB THE LORD BLESSED us with is truly amazing. Let's put into perspective what He actually provided. One day in late December, I was talking to Jon who coaches in our youth baseball league and he was annoyed that a parent commented about him playing "semi-pro ball". To his credit he smiled at the mom and changed the subject because he knew she probably doesn't know any better. Jon has 10 years of minor league playing experience, but has yet to play in the Majors. Most people don't understand how professional baseball works and that each Major League organization can have close to 200 players in their system, not just 25 guys in the big leagues. There are also many quality professional independent league teams out there, which pay their players. Once you get paid to do something, you are called a professional.

So during our conversation I encouraged Jon on how he is in very elite company. I believe the number is less than 1% of all men will play a pro sport during their lifetime. We laughed about what happened and talked about how lucky we are to play and coach baseball for a living and that parents are --- well, parents. On my drive home I started thinking about my new job and some numbers started rushing through my head.

There are 30 organizations in Major League Baseball. Each one has a least 6 minor league teams in their system and they all have a hitting coach. When you add in the MLB hitting coach and roving hitting instructors you get on the average 10 hitting coaches per organization. That's when it hit me. God, you just provided me a job that only 300 other men in the world possess! On top of that, when I thought of how the Giants minor league training facility is only 9 miles from our home and that the job allows me to be with my family every single night, I was overcome with emotion.

The journey seemed like it took forever, but one of the things I learned during this time is that God provides for those who earnestly seek Him. The Lord's timing truly is perfect and when you feel like you are all alone and that He has forgotten about you, realize that He loves you and will never forsake you. Growth happens in the valleys of life, not the mountain tops. During both good and difficult times, we need to keep our lives in perspective and seek God and His perfect will for our lives. Is what you are praying and believing for going to be beneficial for His eternal kingdom, or just yours here on earth?

God is mighty and powerful and our minds put limits on what He can do for us. Pray big and trust Him! In life enjoy the ride, and don't focus only on the destination. You just may miss all of the wonderful scenery He is showing you along the way.

"The count is 2 & 2 to Cabrera. Romo comes set. Here's the pitch --- strike 3 looking! The Giants are the 2012 World Series Champions!!!"

Let's quickly fast forward to the end of my first season with the Giants. Everything has now come full circle in my baseball life. My new team has beaten my old team in the World Series and I'm jumping up and down again in my living room just like I did 28 years ago. Only this time, I'm doing it with my wife in my arms.

Thank You Jesus

Thank you for purchasing this book. If you would like to find out how my first season with the Giants went, please go to the following website address:

www.sevendayfast.com/2012

My Awesome Family - Taleen, Connor (far right) and Bryce

Excited About Daddy's New Job

Derin and I before a Game vs. the AZL Brewers

Coaching First Base in a Game vs. the AZL Dodgers

GLOSSARY OF BIBLE VERSES
New International Version
(Re-printed with permission)

DAY 1

- Trust in the LORD with all your heart and lean not on your own understanding; in all your ways submit to him, and he will make your paths straight.- Proverbs 3:5,6

- "Truly I tell you, if anyone says to this mountain, 'Go, throw yourself into the sea,' and does not doubt in their heart but believes that what they say will happen, it will be done for them. Therefore I tell you, whatever you ask for in prayer, believe that you have received it, and it will be yours.- Mark 11:23,24

- Now may the Lord of peace himself give you peace at all times and in every way. The Lord be with all of you.- 2 Thessalonians 3:16

- Psalm 25

DAY 2

- I seek you with all my heart; do not let me stray from your commands. I have hidden your word in my heart that I might not sin against you.- Psalm 119:10,11

- "Do not judge, and you will not be judged. Do not condemn, and you will not be condemned. Forgive, and you will be forgiven.- Luke 6:37

- The LORD gives strength to his people; the LORD blesses his people with peace.- Psalm 29:11

- Psalm 74

DAY 3

- But he said to me, "My grace is sufficient for you, for my power is made perfect in weakness." Therefore I will boast all the more gladly about my weaknesses, so that Christ's power may rest on me.- 2 Corinthians 12:9

- Do not be anxious about anything, but in every situation, by prayer and petition, with thanksgiving, present your requests to God.- Philippians 4:6

- The LORD is my strength and my shield; my heart trusts in him, and he helps me. My heart leaps for joy, and with my song I praise him.- Psalm 28:7

- Then he continued, "Do not be afraid, Daniel. Since the first day that you set your mind to gain understanding and to humble yourself before your God, your words were heard, and I have come in response to them. But the prince of the Persian kingdom resisted me twenty-one days. Then

Michael, one of the chief princes, came to help me, because I was detained there with the king of Persia.- Daniel 10:12,13

- Psalm 128

DAY 4

- "The LORD is my strength and my defense; he has become my salvation. He is my God, and I will praise him, my father's God, and I will exalt him.- Exodus 15:2

- Blessed is the one who perseveres under trial because, having stood the test, that person will receive the crown of life that the Lord has promised to those who love him.- James 1:12

- No, I strike a blow to my body and make it my slave so that after I have preached to others, I myself will not be disqualified for the prize.- 1 Corinthians 9:27

- Psalm 112

DAY 5

- They will have no fear of bad news; their hearts are steadfast, trusting in the LORD.- Psalm 112:7

- I have not departed from the commands of his lips; I have treasured the words of his mouth more than my daily bread.- Job 23:12
- Now faith is confidence in what we hope for and assurance about what we do not see.- Hebrews 11:1

- Therefore, since we have been justified through faith, we have peace with God through our Lord Jesus Christ, through whom we have gained access by faith into this grace in which we now stand. And we boast in the hope of the glory of God. Not only so, but we also glory in our sufferings, because we know that suffering produces perseverance; perseverance, character; and character, hope. And hope does not put us to shame, because God's love has been poured out into our hearts through the Holy Spirit, who has been given to us.- Romans 5:1-5

- Therefore, I urge you, brothers and sisters, in view of God's mercy, to offer your bodies as a living sacrifice, holy and pleasing to God this is your true and proper worship. ^{2} Do not conform to the pattern of this world, but be transformed by the renewing of your mind. Then you will be able to test and approve what God's will is his good, pleasing and perfect will. For by the grace given me I say to every one of you: Do not think of yourself more highly than you ought, but rather think of yourself with sober judgment, in accordance with the faith God has distributed to each of you. For just as each of us has one body with many members, and these members do not all have the same function, so in Christ we, though many, form one body, and each member belongs to all the others. We have different gifts, according to the grace given to each of us. If your gift is prophesying, then prophesy in accordance with your faith; if it is serving, then serve; if it is teaching, then teach; if it is to encourage, then give encouragement; if it is giving, then give generously; if it is to lead, do it diligently; if it is to show mercy, do it cheerfully- Romans 12:1-8

DAY 6

- For I know the plans I have for you," declares the LORD, "plans to prosper you and not to harm you, plans to give you hope and a future.- Jeremiah 29:11

- I pray that the eyes of your heart may be enlightened in order that you may know the hope to which he has called you, the riches of his glorious inheritance in his holy people- Ephesians 1:18

- Have I not commanded you? Be strong and courageous. Do not be afraid; do not be discouraged, for the LORD your God will be with you wherever you go."- Joshua 1:9

- Psalm 27

DAY 7

- Do you not know that your bodies are temples of the Holy Spirit, who is in you, whom you have received from God? You are not your own; you were bought at a price. Therefore honor God with your bodies.- 1 Corinthians 19,20

- You will keep in perfect peace those whose minds are steadfast, because they trust in you. Trust in the LORD forever, for the LORD, the LORD himself, is the Rock eternal- Isaiah 26:3,4

- I pray that out of his glorious riches he may strengthen you with power through his Spirit in your inner being- Ephesians 3:16

- I can do all this through him who gives me strength.- Philippians 4:13

- Then the word of the LORD came to Elijah: "Leave here, turn eastward and hide in the Kerith Ravine, east of the Jordan. You will drink from the brook, and I have directed the ravens to supply you with food there. So he did what the LORD had told him. He went to the Kerith Ravine, east of the Jordan, and stayed there. The ravens brought him bread and meat in the morning and bread and meat in the evening, and he drank from the brook.- 1 Kings 17: 2-6

- "When you fast, do not look somber as the hypocrites do, for they disfigure their faces to show others they are fasting. Truly I tell you, they have received their reward in full. But when you fast, put oil on your head and wash your face, so that it will not be obvious to others that you are fasting, but only to your Father, who is unseen; and your Father, who sees what is done in secret, will reward you.- Matthew 6:16-18

- Psalm 28

AFTER THE FAST

- Therefore do not worry about tomorrow, for tomorrow will worry about itself. Each day has enough trouble of its own.- Matthew 6:34

ABOUT THE AUTHOR

Billy Horton is a current minor league hitting coach with the San Francisco Giants. He is a former professional baseball player as well as the Founder, President and Director of Baseball Operations for Cactus Athletic Camps and the Arizona Baseball League. These two organizations provide professional baseball and exercise training for youth ages 8 to 18 years old in the greater Phoenix, AZ area. Billy also founded Teen Impact, a youth athletic organization that brings in professional Christian athletes to speak to teenage athletes as well as provide them with free dinner and bibles.

Even though he was cut his freshman year in high school, he eventually earned a college baseball scholarship and played in the Minor Leagues from 1997-2000. Billy has 15 years of coaching experience and has worked in nearly every level of the game from youth baseball up to the professional ranks. He has been on the board of directors for multiple organizations and currently serves on the board for the Fellowship of Christian Athletes Baseball Division as well as Unashamed Athletes.

Billy lives in Scottsdale, AZ with his beautiful wife Taleen and his two incredible sons, Connor and Bryce. Providing for them and being a good witness for Christ are the only two things that he truly cares about, and they are the reason this book became a reality. He attends Impact Church, a non-denominational Christian church in Scottsdale.

╫RICHER Press
An Imprint of Richer Life, LLC

RICHER Press is a full service, specialty Trade publisher whose sole goal is to *shape thoughts and change lives for the better.* All of the books, eBooks and digital media we publish, distribute and market embrace our commitment to help maximize opportunities for personal growth and professional achievement.

To learn more visit
www.richerlifeassociates.com.

CPSIA information can be obtained at www.ICGtesting.com
Printed in the USA
BVOW100739060213

312504BV00003B/4/P